Explore
ASIA

Bobbie Kalman & Rebecca Sjonger

Crabtree Publishing Company

www.crabtreebooks.com

Created by Bobbie Kalman

Dedicated by Heather Fitzpatrick
To my dear friends Ljiljana and Nihad Selimović

Editor-in-Chief
Bobbie Kalman

Writing team
Bobbie Kalman
Rebecca Sjonger

Substantive editor
Kelley MacAulay

Editors
Molly Aloian
Michael Hodge
Kathryn Smithyman

Photo research
Crystal Foxton

Design
Katherine Kantor

Production coordinator
Heather Fitzpatrick

Prepress technician
Nancy Johnson

Consultant
Craig ZumBrunnen, Ph.D., Department of Geography
and Henry M. Jackson School of International Studies,
University of Washington

Illustrations
Barbara Bedell: page 19
Katherine Kantor: pages 5 (top), 11 (map and leopard), 14 (left), 23
Robert MacGregor: front cover (map), back cover (map), pages 6, 7, 14 (right),
    16 (top), 17 (bottom), 18 (top), 20 (bottom left), 21 (middle), 22 (map)
Vanessa Parson-Robbs: pages 9, 24, 26 (top), 28 (map), 30 (map), 31 (maps)
Bonna Rouse: pages 11 (turtle), 20 (flower)
Margaret Amy Salter: pages 11 (flowers), 13 (snowflakes), 15, 17 (top),
    20 (marmot), 21 (top)

Photographs
© Bryan & Cherry Alexander/Arcticphoto.com: page 21 (bottom)
Corbis: © China Photo/Reuters: page 29; © Carl & Ann Purcell: page 19
Dreamstime.com: Nasrulla Adnan: page 8; Marcus Brown: page 31 (bottom)
iStockphoto.com: front cover, back cover (bottom), pages 1, 5 (bottom), 13, 15,
    17, 20 (top), 25, 26 (bottom)
© Lynn M. Stone/naturepl.com: page 22
© Shutterstock: Galina Barskaya: page 27; Wong Yick Heng: page 24;
    Marc C. Johnson: page 10
Other images by Corbis, Corel, Digital Stock, Digital Vision, and Photodisc

Library and Archives Canada Cataloguing in Publication

Kalman, Bobbie, 1947-
    Explore Asia / Bobbie Kalman & Rebecca Sjonger.

(Explore the continents)
Includes index.
ISBN 978-0-7787-3072-9 (bound)
ISBN 978-0-7787-3086-6 (pbk.)

    1. Asia--Geography--Juvenile literature. I. Sjonger, Rebecca
II. Title. III. Series.

DS5.K34 2007   j915   C2007-900724-4

Library of Congress Cataloging-in-Publication Data

Kalman, Bobbie.
    Explore Asia / Bobbie Kalman & Rebecca Sjonger.
        p. cm. -- (Explore the continents)
    Includes index.
    ISBN-13: 978-0-7787-3072-9 (rlb)
    ISBN-10: 0-7787-3072-7 (rlb)
    ISBN-13: 978-0-7787-3086-6 (pb)
    ISBN-10: 0-7787-3086-7 (pb)
    1. Asia--Juvenile literature. I. Sjonger, Rebecca. II. Title.
III. Series.
    DS5.K17 2007
    915--dc22

                                                2007003467

Crabtree Publishing Company

www.crabtreebooks.com   1-800-387-7650

Published in Canada
Crabtree Publishing
616 Welland Ave.
St. Catharines, Ontario
L2M 5V6

Published in the United States
Crabtree Publishing
PMB16A
350 Fifth Ave., Suite 3308
New York, NY 10118

Published in the United Kingdom
Crabtree Publishing
White Cross Mills
High Town, Lancaster
LA1 4XS

Published in Australia
Crabtree Publishing
386 Mt. Alexander Rd.
Ascot Vale (Melbourne)
VIC 3032

Contents

Continents and oceans

Continents are huge areas of land on Earth. There are seven continents. From largest to smallest, the seven continents are Asia, Africa, North America, South America, Antarctica, Europe, and Australia/Oceania. This book is about the continent of Asia.

Asia is the largest continent on Earth!

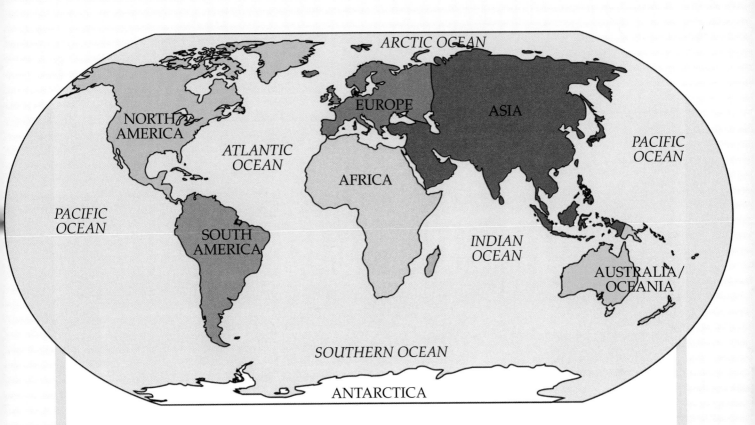

Map labels: ARCTIC OCEAN, NORTH AMERICA, EUROPE, ASIA, ATLANTIC OCEAN, PACIFIC OCEAN, AFRICA, PACIFIC OCEAN, SOUTH AMERICA, INDIAN OCEAN, AUSTRALIA/OCEANIA, SOUTHERN OCEAN, ANTARCTICA

Huge areas of water

There are five **oceans** on Earth. Oceans are the largest areas of water on Earth. The oceans are different sizes. From largest to smallest, the five oceans are the Pacific Ocean, the Atlantic Ocean, the Indian Ocean, the Southern Ocean, and the Arctic Ocean. Find the seven continents and the five oceans on the map above.

Most of the Indian Ocean has warm, clear waters.

Directions on Earth

North, south, east, and west are the four main **directions** on Earth. The **North Pole** is at the top of Earth. The **South Pole** is at the bottom of Earth. Near the North Pole and the South Pole, the weather is always cold.

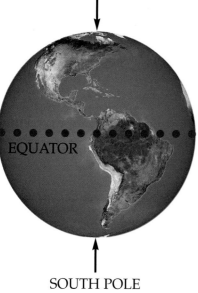

NORTH POLE

N

W ← ✦ → E

S

EQUATOR

EQUATOR

SOUTH POLE

Dividing Earth

There is an imaginary line around Earth. The line is called the **equator**. The equator goes around Earth's center. It divides Earth into two equal halves. Near the equator, the weather is hot all year long.

ASIA

The top half

The top half of Earth is called the **Northern Hemisphere**. It goes from the equator to the North Pole. Most of Asia is above the equator. It is in the Northern Hemisphere.

The bottom half

The bottom half of Earth is called the **Southern Hemisphere**. It goes from the equator to the South Pole. Part of Asia is below the equator. It is in the Southern Hemisphere.

Countries in Asia

There are 50 **countries** in Asia. A country is a part of a continent. A country has **borders**. Borders are the areas where one country ends and another country begins. A country is run by a group of people. This group of people is called the **government**.

*Maldives is the smallest country in Asia. It is made up of a group of **islands**. An island is land that is surrounded by water. This picture shows one of the Maldives islands.*

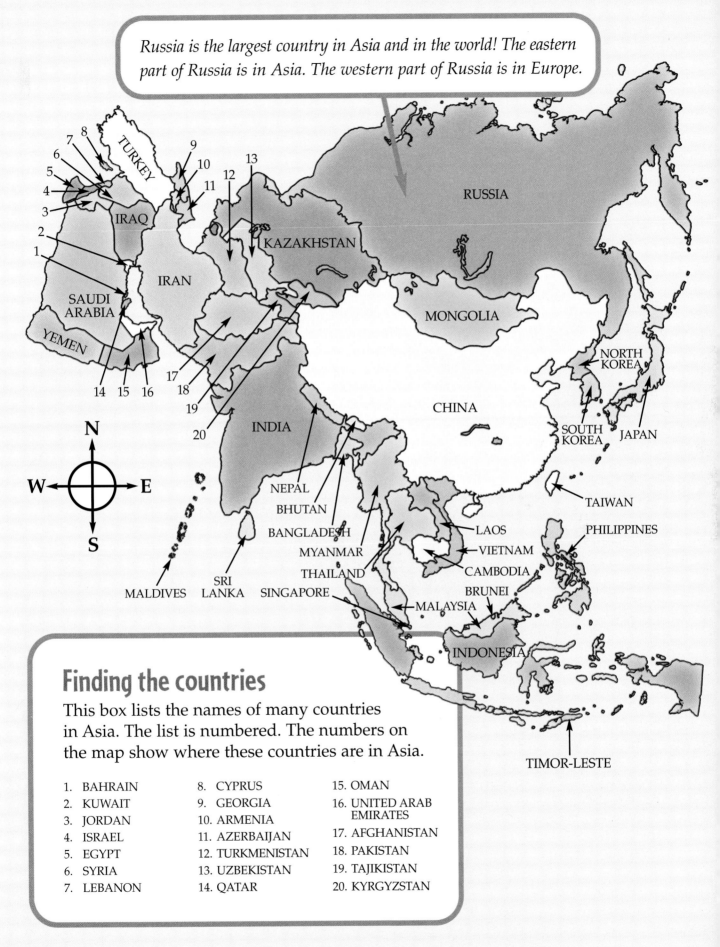

Russia is the largest country in Asia and in the world! The eastern part of Russia is in Asia. The western part of Russia is in Europe.

RUSSIA

TURKEY

IRAQ

IRAN

KAZAKHSTAN

MONGOLIA

SAUDI ARABIA

YEMEN

CHINA

NORTH KOREA

SOUTH KOREA

JAPAN

INDIA

TAIWAN

NEPAL

BHUTAN

BANGLADESH

MYANMAR

THAILAND

SINGAPORE

MALDIVES

SRI LANKA

LAOS

VIETNAM

CAMBODIA

BRUNEI

MALAYSIA

PHILIPPINES

INDONESIA

TIMOR-LESTE

N
W E
S

Finding the countries

This box lists the names of many countries in Asia. The list is numbered. The numbers on the map show where these countries are in Asia.

1. BAHRAIN
2. KUWAIT
3. JORDAN
4. ISRAEL
5. EGYPT
6. SYRIA
7. LEBANON
8. CYPRUS
9. GEORGIA
10. ARMENIA
11. AZERBAIJAN
12. TURKMENISTAN
13. UZBEKISTAN
14. QATAR
15. OMAN
16. UNITED ARAB EMIRATES
17. AFGHANISTAN
18. PAKISTAN
19. TAJIKISTAN
20. KYRGYZSTAN

9

Six regions in Asia

Asia is a huge continent! It is so big that some people group the countries together into six **regions**. The six regions are listed below.

1. Northern Asia
2. Central Asia
3. Western Asia
4. Southern Asia
5. Eastern Asia
6. Southeastern Asia

Western Asia is often called "the Middle East." This picture shows part of Oman. Oman is a country in Western Asia.

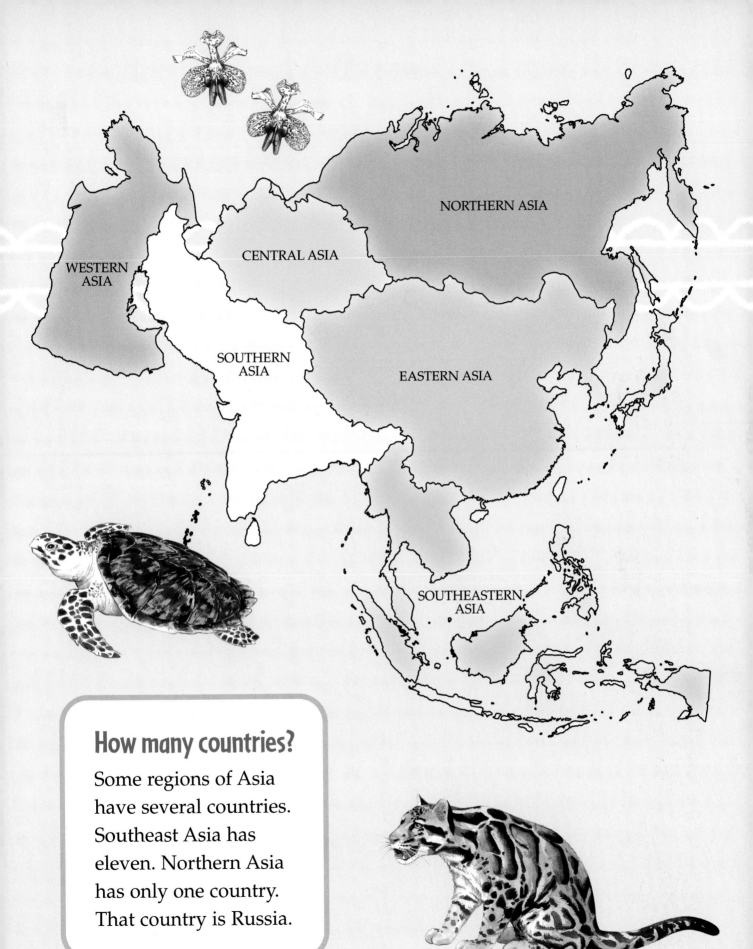

NORTHERN ASIA

CENTRAL ASIA

WESTERN
ASIA

SOUTHERN
ASIA

EASTERN ASIA

SOUTHEASTERN
ASIA

How many countries?

Some regions of Asia
have several countries.
Southeast Asia has
eleven. Northern Asia
has only one country.
That country is Russia.

Climate

The **climate** is not the same in all the regions of Asia. Climate is the kind of weather that an area usually has in each season. Some regions of Asia are closer to the North Pole than they are to the equator. These regions are cold and snowy much of the year. Northern Asia has long cold winters and short cool summers. Other regions of Asia are closer to the equator than they are to the North Pole. These regions are warm all year long.

Southeastern Asia is near the equator. It is always warm there. This picture shows part of Indonesia. Indonesia is in Southeastern Asia.

Rain and snow

In some regions of Asia, it rains a lot. Southern Asia, Eastern Asia, and Southeastern Asia get a lot of rain. Other regions of Asia get very little rain. Western Asia and Central Asia are dry regions. Northern Asia is very cold for most of the year. It gets some snow, but not a lot, because snow does not fall in very cold weather.

Snow sometimes falls in other regions of Asia. This picture shows snow in Japan. Japan is in Eastern Asia.

Waterways in Asia

Three oceans touch Asia's **coasts**. A coast is the part of land that meets an ocean. The Arctic Ocean is along the northern coasts of Asia. The Pacific Ocean is along the eastern coasts of Asia. The Indian Ocean is along the southern coasts of Asia. There are also many **seas** along Asia's coasts. A sea is a small area of ocean with land around it.

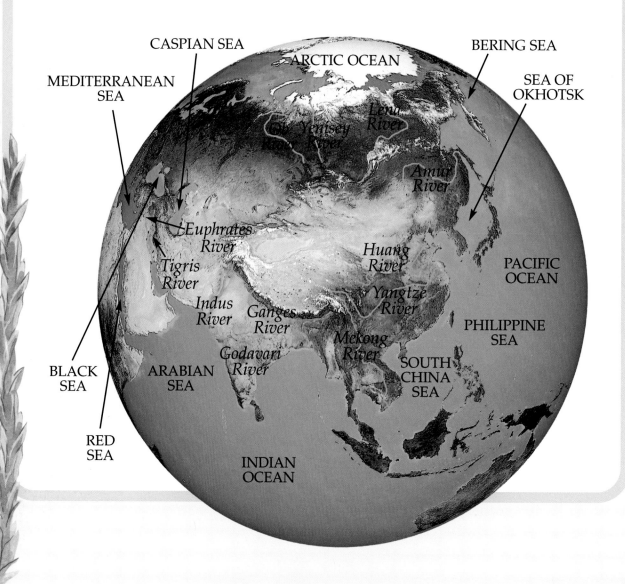

CASPIAN SEA

MEDITERRANEAN SEA

BERING SEA

SEA OF OKHOTSK

ARCTIC OCEAN

Lena River

Ob' Yenisey River

Amur River

Euphrates River

Huang River

PACIFIC OCEAN

Tigris River

Indus River

Ganges River

Yangtze River

PHILIPPINE SEA

Mekong River

BLACK SEA

ARABIAN SEA

Godavari River

SOUTH CHINA SEA

RED SEA

INDIAN OCEAN

Looking at lakes

There are large **lakes** in Asia. A lake is an area of water that is surrounded by land. The Caspian Sea is a lake in Asia. It is the largest lake on Earth! Most lakes have **fresh water**. Fresh water has very little salt in it. The Caspian Sea is a lake with **salt water**. There is a lot of salt in salt water.

*There are also many **rivers** in Asia. The Yangtze River is in China. It is one of the longest rivers in the world.*

The land in Asia

Asia has many **mountains**. Mountains are tall areas of land. They have steep sides. A mountain is a kind of **landform**. Other landforms are low hills, flat **steppes**, and narrow or wide **valleys**.

The brown areas on this map show where some mountains are in Asia.

MOUNT FUJI

mountains

Snow leopards live on mountains in Central Asia.

Volcanoes

There are openings on the tops of some mountains. Mountains that have openings on their tops are called **volcanoes**. Smoke, ash, and **lava** sometimes come out of a volcano's opening. There are many volcanoes in Asia.

Mount Fuji is one of the most famous volcanoes on Earth. It is in Japan.

ARABIAN PENINSULA

Peninsulas

Asia has many **peninsulas**. A peninsula is land that sticks out into water. It is connected to a larger piece of land.

The Arabian Peninsula is in Western Asia. It is the largest peninsula on Earth.

Two types of deserts

There are big **deserts** in Asia. Most deserts are dry and hot, but some deserts are dry and cold. Asia's hot deserts are in Western Asia, Southern Asia, and Central Asia. The cold deserts are in Eastern Asia.

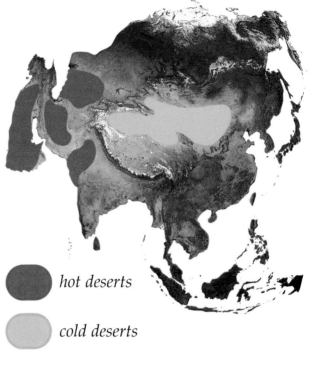

hot deserts

cold deserts

Plants need water to stay alive. Plants cannot grow in most deserts. Deserts are too dry. There is a river in this sandy desert. Plants grow beside the river, where they can get the water they need.

Few animals

Few animals live in Asia's deserts. There is not enough water for most animals to stay alive. Camels live in Asia's deserts. Camels drink huge amounts of water and store it in their bodies. After drinking, camels do not need to drink again for a long time.

The word "Bedouin" means "people who live in the desert."

Desert people

Many people who live in Asian deserts are **Bedouins**. Bedouins travel from place to place. They must travel to find enough water to drink and food to eat.

Flat steppes

Grasslands grow around many of Asia's deserts. Grasslands are large areas where the land is mainly flat. Many kinds of grasses and some wildflowers grow on grasslands. In Asia, grasslands are called **steppes**. Poppies are wildflowers that grow on Asian steppes.

Very few trees grow on steppes.

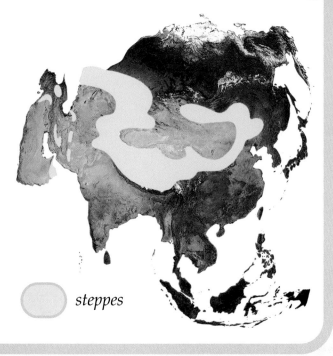

steppes

Fast fact

Bobak marmots live on the steppes in Asia. They eat the grasses that grow there.

Frozen tundra

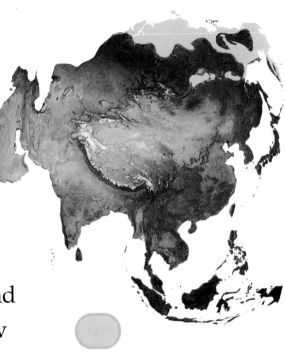

Russia is the most northern country in Asia. It is cold and dry in northern Russia. The land there is mainly flat. This flat, cold land is called the **tundra**. The tundra is frozen in winter. It is covered with snow. In summer, the top layer of ground thaws. A few small plants grow on the tundra in summer.

tundra

Some people live on the tundra. They travel over the snow on sleds. Reindeer pull the sleds.

Forests full of trees

There are **forests** in Asia. Forests are areas where many trees grow. In Northern Asia, forests are made up mainly of **coniferous trees**. Coniferous trees have leaves shaped like needles. In warmer parts of Asia, other forests grow. These forests have both coniferous and **broadleaved trees**. Broadleaved trees have wide, flat leaves.

forests

Bamboo forests are made up of bamboo plants. These forests grow in Eastern Asia. Giant pandas live in the forests and eat the bamboo plants.

Rainy forests

Tropical rain forests grow in Southeastern Asia. These rain forests grow in places with hot, wet climates. Many kinds of animals live in the tropical rain forests in Southeastern Asia.

Orangutans live in tropical rain forests in Asia.

Life in rural areas

Close to four billion people live in Asia!
Most Asian people live in **rural areas**.
A rural area is a place outside a city
or a town. Rural people in Asia live
in different kinds of homes. Many
people in Central Asia live in **yurts**.
A yurt is a tentlike home.

yurt

In Cambodia, some people live in a group of wooden homes that float on water. The homes float on Tonle Sap Lake. Most of the people who live there catch fish to eat.

Market foods

Many people in rural Asia grow their own food to eat. Some people buy food in **markets**. A market is a group of shops that sells fruits, vegetables, and fish. Clothes and other items are also sold in markets.

This woman is selling fruits and vegetables at a market in Malaysia.

Life in urban areas

Cities and towns are called **urban areas**. Hundreds of millions of people live in Asia's biggest cities. Some of the most crowded Asian cities are Tokyo in Japan and Mumbai in India.

This map shows some of the cities in Asia.

ISTANBUL
YEKATERINBURG
OMSK
NOVOSIBIRSK
TEHRAN
TOKYO
BEIJING
LAHORE
OSAKA
KARACHI
WUHAN
SHANGHAI
DELHI
DHAKA
MUMBAI
HONG KONG
CALCUTTA
BANGALORE
MANILA
BANGKOK
JAKARTA

Many people in Asia move from rural areas to urban areas. They move to find jobs, but jobs are hard to find. Without jobs, some families must live in poorly made homes.

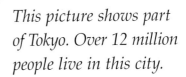

This picture shows part of Tokyo. Over 12 million people live in this city.

Valuable resources

There is a lot of oil in the ground in Asia. Oil is a **natural resource**. Natural resources are materials found in nature. People sell natural resources to make money. Oil is a **valuable** natural resource. Countries from all over the world buy oil from Asia. The locations of some of Asia's natural resources are shown on this map.

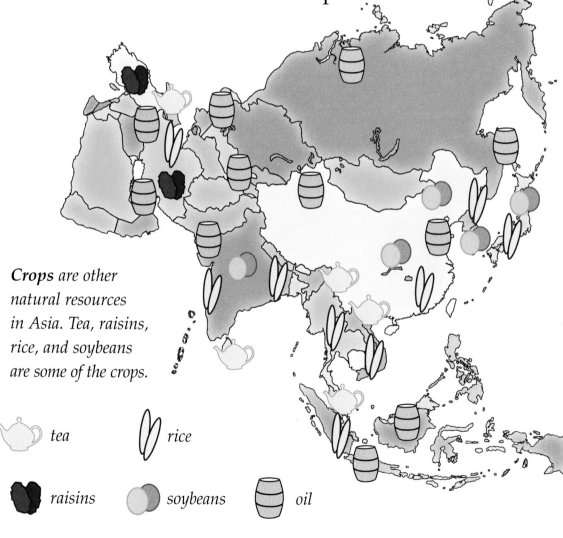

Crops are other natural resources in Asia. Tea, raisins, rice, and soybeans are some of the crops.

tea

rice

raisins   soybeans   oil

Crop killers

There are often **tropical storms** in Asia. Tropical storms are rainstorms with strong winds. They can cause **floods**. Floods are deep waters on land that is usually dry. Strong winds and floods often damage crops. Farmers cannot sell damaged crops. When crops are damaged, farmers cannot make enough money to support their families.

This family's crops have been damaged by flood waters.

Postcards from Asia

Many **tourists** from all over the world visit Asia each year. A tourist is a person who visits a place for fun. Some of the most popular tourist places in Asia are shown here.

The Great Wall of China is made up of a number of stone walls. The walls were built long ago to protect northern China from enemies. Together, the walls are about 1,500 miles (2,414 km) long! Parts of some walls are over 2,000 years old.

India's Taj Mahal is a beautiful **tomb** that was built in the mid 1600s. Emperor Shah Jahan had it built after the death of his wife, Mumatz Mahal.

Many people visit the interesting **stupas** in Myanmar. Stupas are special **Buddhist** buildings.

Glossary

Note: Boldfaced words that are defined in the text may not appear in the glossary.

Buddhist A person who follows the teachings of the Buddha; describes something that is part of a religion called Buddhism

crops Plants that people grow for food

desert A hot, dry area that receives less than 10 inches (25 cm) of rain each year

lava Hot liquid rock that shoots out of volcanoes

region One of six large areas into which Asia is divided

river A large area of water that flows into an ocean, a lake, or another river

steppe A flat area of land where many grasses grow

tomb A place in which people are buried after they die

tropical rain forest A forest that grows in an area near the equator that receives at least 100 inches (254 cm) of rain each year

valley A low area of land between mountains

valuable Describes something that is worth a lot of money or is treasured by people

Index

Printed in the U.S.A.